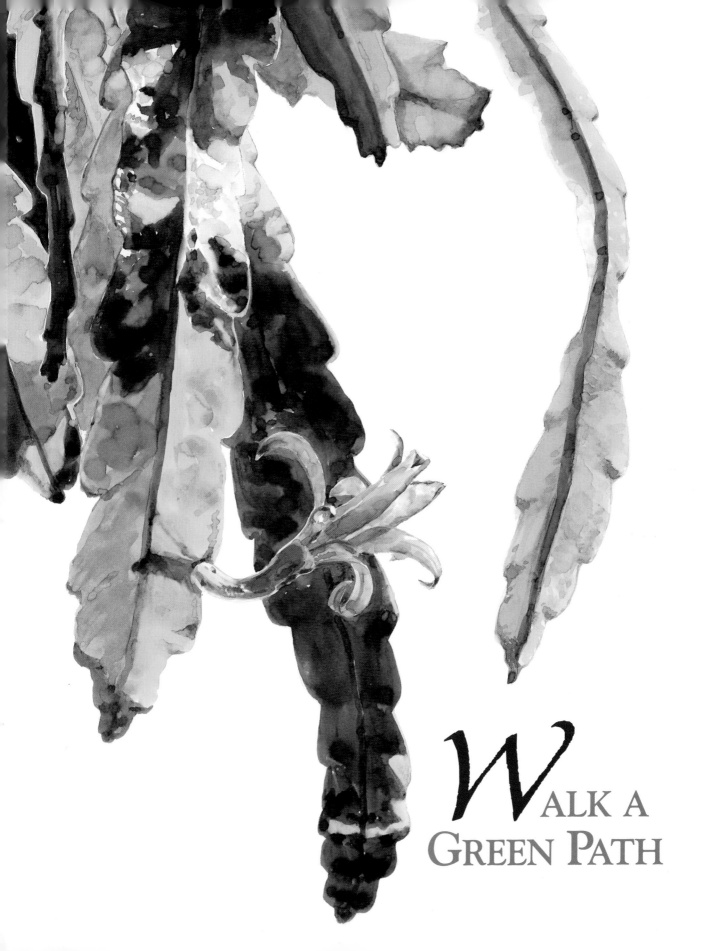

Walk a
Green Path

Walk a Green Path

Betsy Lewin

LOTHROP, LEE & SHEPARD BOOKS
NEW YORK

Bird-of-Paradise

The bird-of-paradise was not in bloom.
There was an embarrassed silence about it,
like someone searching for the right word.
I waited. Finally it spoke to me in another voice—
its green voice.

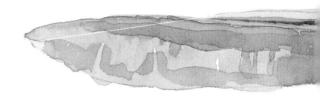

When this plant does bloom, it blooms in the
Brooklyn Botanic Garden in Brooklyn,
New York, where I painted it.

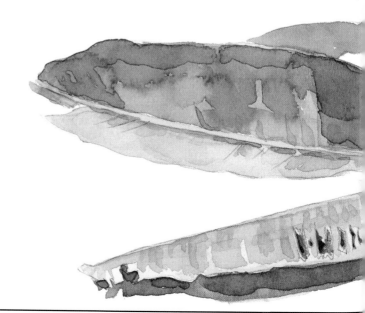

Moonvine

Soft white flowers glow in a green night.
At dawn a barred owl sails without sound to its bed.
Soon the moonflowers will be tight white fists.

*These moonvine flowers in the Florida Everglades
open at twilight and close after dawn. The barred
owl sometimes hunts during the day, but I like
to think that this one went to bed with the
moonflowers.*

Moonflowers
B Erwin '84

Traveler's-Tree

Fanned stems rise like organ pipes,
bursting into a crescendo of leaves.

*The traveler's-tree got its name because the water that collects at the
base of its leaves often quenched the thirst of a desert traveler. I
painted this one in Hawaii.*

Houseplants

In spring I take them
from their winter windows
out to the backyard
to coax the summer.

*The roots of the large maple tree
in my backyard strangle
everything I try to plant
in the ground. I forgive it,
though, because of the
glorious shade it provides.*

Lake Forest

I stand at the edge of a lake,
longing to enter the tiny forest
that sprouts from the stump
of a drowned tree.

*The trails in New York's Harriman State Park lead
to wonderful surprises such as Lake Skenonto on
the Victory Trail.*

Canoe Trail

I drift in a world where
the sky is green,
the clouds are green,
and the trees are upside down.

*The Bear Lake Canoe Trail in
the Florida Everglades is part of
a canal dug in the 1920s. Its
waters flow slowly through
the mangroves into Florida Bay.*

Victoria Regina

Four feet across and rimmed with thorns,
the Victoria Regina lily pad
looks like a giant pie shell
and can keep a child afloat.
It has no enemies until it begins to die—
then it's food for fish.

*I saw these lily pads in the Parc National
across the Amazon River from Manaus,
a city of one million people smack in the middle
of the Brazilian rain forest.*

Fern Ruín

Deep in the rain forest,
jaguars lurk,
parrots call,
ancient Mayans climb stone steps
to jungle cities.
All this
beneath a supermarket fern
atop a chunk of lintel.

*My backyard is full of seashells, rocks that are special
to me, and chunks of stone ornaments from demolished
nineteenth-century buildings.*

Captain Don's Garden

An old deep-sea diver,
ship captain, swashbuckler,
moved to a desert island just like him—
brown, thorny, tough, beautiful—
and made this green garden.

*Sailing to Bonaire in the Netherlands Antilles
for the first time in 1962, Captain
Don Stewart called it an enchanted island:
"Somehow that day I sensed my anchor
was never again to leave this shore."
He has been instrumental in protecting
the environment of the island and its
coral reefs.*

Capt. Don's Garden
B Lewin '89

Backyard Angel

I wonder if, when I'm not there,
he talks to the pill bugs, the periwinkle,
and the Little People?

*My cat Bones spent hours curled in the garden. He's gone now,
but his soul lingers in the concrete angel.*

Lotus

*L*otus.
The word floats from my tongue,
whispers in my ears.
In the leafy dream below the blossom,
I see ancient Egypt.

Pharaohs gazed upon the sacred lotus five thousand years
ago. This one stands in the Brooklyn Botanic Garden.

Mr. Dott

Mr. Dott—
old footballer,
sugarcane grower
between a rain forest and the sea—
knows green.
Plants it.
Lives it.

*Among the plants in Mr. Dott's garden in
Australia's Pioneer Valley is one called Monstera
deliciosa. Each of its bite-size fruits has a
different flavor. One might taste like a cherry,
another like a banana, an orange, or a coconut.*

The Holly Bench

I left the corner luncheonette
and took my lemonade across the street.
Sitting in the walled garden,
I poked the straw through the lid.
Gone—the August heat,
the city's metal voice.

*This Brooklyn garden was created from a
garbage-strewn lot by neighborhood
volunteers. It was officially opened in a
ribbon-cutting ceremony on the first
Earth Day on April 22, 1970, by Mayor
John V. Lindsay.*

Rain Forest

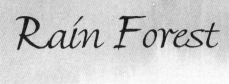

The rain forest holds its breath,
waiting for the downpour.

Itatiaia (ee-tah-chee-i-yah) is the last stand of Atlantic
coastal rain forest in Brazil. If it goes, there is no more.

for Ed Grimm

The painting on the cover is of the Eungella rain forest in Australia.
The flower pictured on the endpapers is a water lily
on the Boteti River in Botswana.
The flower on the half title is a Christmas cactus,
and the plant on the title page is a Seloum, both houseplants of mine.
—Betsy Lewin

The illustrations in this book were done in water color paints.
The display type was set in Goudy Bold and Fine Hand.
The text was set in Goudy. Printed and bound by South China.
Production supervision by Esilda Kerr. Designed by Robin Ballard.

Inquiries should be addressed to
Lothrop, Lee & Shepard Books, a division of William Morrow & Company, Inc.,
1350 Avenue of the Americas, New York, New York 10019.
Printed in Hong Kong

First Edition   1 2 3 4 5 6 7 8 9 10

Library of Congress Cataloging in Publication Data
Lewin, Betsy. Walk a green path / by Betsy Lewin.
p.   cm. ISBN 0-688-13425-4.
1. Plants—Juvenile literature. 2. Natural history—Juvenile literature.
3. Gardens—Juvenile literature. [1. Gardens. 2. Plants. 3. Nature.]
1. Title. QK49.L59 1995 581—dc20
94-14824 CIP AC